THE BOAZ BLESSING

THE BOAZ BLESSING

UNDERSTANDING THE POWER OF COVENANT

BRUCE WIKE

TATE PUBLISHING
AND ENTERPRISES, LLC

Published by Tate Publishing & Enterprises, LLC
127 E. Trade Center Terrace | Mustang, Oklahoma 73064 USA
1.888.361.9473 | www.tatepublishing.com

Tate Publishing is committed to excellence in the publishing industry. The company reflects the philosophy established by the founders, based on Psalm 68:11,
"The Lord gave the word and great was the company of those who published it."

Book design copyright © 2014 by Tate Publishing, LLC. All rights reserved.
Cover design by Gian philipp Rufin
Interior design by Gram Telen

Published in the United States of America

ISBN: 978-1-63063-557-2
1. Religion / Christian Life / General
2. Religion / Christian Life / Spiritual Growth
14.01.27

DEDICATION

This book is dedicated to my loving wife Lisa and my daughters Brittany DeHart and her family, Cassie Hood and her family, and Kaelie Wike. This dedication extends to my parents, Monte and Noma Wike and to all those who have poured into my life through the years to teach me the ways of God.

CONTENTS

ACKNOWLEDGMENTS

I am deeply indebted to those without whose help and encouragement this project would have never been completed. First of all, I want to thank my wonderful wife, Lisa, for her undying support and belief in both me and the writing of this book. I wish also to thank my three daughters, Brittany, Cassie, and Kaelie for their continual encouragement. And a thank you goes to my father, Rev. Monte Wike, for providing the first reading and edit of this project.

The efforts of my editor, Candace Gleghorn, have been a greater blessing than I have words to express. She took a rough, poorly written manuscript, and helped me say what needed to be said. I am truly grateful for her work and diligence on this book.

During the initial writing of the book, I shared with a local businessman what I was doing. Every time he saw me, he questioned me about the book and its progress. It was his continual persuasion that motivated me to actually complete the project and get it in print. Thank you, Mike Mitchell, for your friendship.

Lastly, I want to express my appreciation to my church family at Longview Metro Church and Senior Pastors Rob and Freda Parsons for their encouragement as well. I taught this material to them as I was writing it. The opportunity to share this with them is extremely rewarding.

FOREWORD

Some would argue today whether or not God still speaks to man. Some would argue the extent of God's power. Others wonder if God is still empowering the lives of people to carry out His will on earth.

Let me be quick to say that I believe beyond all measure of doubt that God still speaks to mankind. I believe God is all-powerful, and I am fully persuaded that He continues to empower the lives of those who desire to pursue a relationship with Him.

For too long the Church has taught, and has *been* taught that we are supposed to be religious. Christianity is not about *practicing religion*, rather it is about building a life-long relationship with God that grows and matures as we live for Him.

What we will discover as we pursue the person, the presence, and the power of God is that He will equip us for the purpose to which He has called us. He has a destiny for each of us, and He has the necessary power and resources to help us fulfill that destiny.

I have been blessed in my life to have had the pleasure of serving the body of Christ in many different capacities. I began serving in church as a small boy singing, playing the piano, and playing the trombone. At the age of nineteen, I began traveling doing concerts at churches in the southern part of our nation. At twenty, I was asked to be the youth pastor in Mineral Wells, Texas. At twenty-one, I moved to Tyler, Texas to accept a Youth Pastor position. During my nearly eleven years there, in addition to serving as youth pastor, I worked in the Day Care office, led the choir, led the congregational music, edited the weekly TV broadcast, and taught a Sunday School class. It was during those years that I discovered a passion for writing.

Later, I served as an evangelist, a senior pastor, and then as an associate pastor; a role I continue to fill at the time of this writing.

In April of 2009, while attending our church's early morning prayer meeting, the Lord began to deal with me about Boaz and the book of Ruth. I had read the book of Ruth a number of times; however, it was not one of those books I drew a great amount of strength from. I felt very strongly in my spirit that I needed to reread the book of Ruth and that there were things that the Holy Spirit wanted to show me. As I was reading, the Lord began to show me small things. I went back to prayer and asked the Holy Spirit to reveal to me what He wanted me to see. He impressed on me quite strongly to begin writing a book from the book of Ruth and to call it *The Boaz Blessing*.

As the Lord began dealing with me, I looked at my schedule. I was in the busiest part of my year. I was currently trying to finish another book I was writing; and in addition, we were making preparations to be first-time grandparents. Life was busy to say the least, but I started out of obedience.

What you will read in this book comes out of a deep desire to please God and to help others find their destiny in God.

There are some powerful spiritual principles found in this book that are revealed through the life of Boaz that I believe God is wanting the Body of Christ to rediscover and apply to their own lives.

May you be blessed as you read.

—Bruce Wike

THE MOAB MOMENT

Regardless of who you are, what kind of background you came from, or what your life has become, you have had the experience of doing something for all the right reasons and seeing that decision not working out. These are the times when we really question God. Our prayer time is filled with statements like: "God, I don't understand why bad things are happening. My heart was pure in my decision making, my motive was pure but my whole world is crumbling. What is going on?"

These are the times when your faith is tested, your grit and determination is tried, and your relationships are put to the test. These are those times that make you or break you. These are those times when you either grow up or throw in the towel. These are the times that reveal your character and shape your destiny.

I would love to tell you that my life has been so amazing that I cannot relate to such events but that would not be true. I know firsthand the difficulty that comes from walking through what I will refer to in this chapter as a *Moab moment*. Moab moments are those seasons in your life that test every fiber of your being.

In the summer of 2001, after pastoring a great church in East Texas for seven years, we felt like it was time to go and see what the Lord would do through us in another location. We loaded up our belongings, left a place that even with its challenges in our last year of ministry was still a comfortable place for our family. It was a place where we had put down roots, built relationships, and had grown a ministry. It was a hard decision, but we felt like it was God's will, so we left to pastor a church in South Texas.

We were excited about living on the coast of Texas. We were looking forward to new experiences and new opportunities. But it turned out to be a Moab moment in our lives. Nothing was as it appeared to be. The church was in major conflict, the finances were shrinking, there was a power struggle with some of the leaders, and the lack of unity was overwhelming.

We knew God wanted to use us to bring a spirit of revival to them, but they refused to be led, and literally within months, we knew we could no longer stay. It put a strain on my children and my wife. I knew I had to choose between the well-being of my family and trying to revive Moab. I chose my family, and we relocated back to East Texas.

Those Moab moments can feel more like a lifetime than mere moments, because they exact such a heavy price from you as you go through them.

Moab was a place of sin, idolatry, and perversion. It was bordered on the west by the Dead Sea and the east by Ammon and the Arabian Desert. It is a metaphor for a dry season or a wilderness experience in your life. If you will let

Him, God will order your steps even when you are going through a Moab moment. It was in Moab that Naomi's son met and married Ruth who would be in the lineage of Christ.

The contrast to Moab is Bethlehem. Bethlehem was in the land of Judah. Judah literally means *praise*. Even though Naomi and her family left Bethlehem for all the right reasons; they were trying to provide for their family—the place they went to that they thought would bring provision, brought death. Naomi's husband died, her two sons-in-law died, she had no inheritance in the land of Moab, and no family on which to lean for encouragement. If she wanted to live there was but one choice, and that was to return to Judah.

I personally believe her life began to change when she made the decision to begin the journey back toward Judah. The blessing of Boaz that would eventually touch Naomi's life and the life of Ruth was there waiting for them, but first they had to initiate their pursuit of praise.

The destiny God has for you is not to die in Moab. Scripture is clear when God said, "The thief cometh not but for to kill, and to steal, and to destroy; I have come that they might have life, and that they might have it more abundantly" (John 10:10 KJV). God's will for you is that you have a full, abundant, overflowing life; A life without measure; A life that displays His goodness to you and His blessings upon you; A life of health, financial overflow, and joy. That is the kind of life that comes from being in the place where God has called you to be. It is in that place of God's perfect will that His anointing flows freely in your life.

The anointing of God's Spirit will never be released upon you or through you apart from your pursuit of praise. Praise is simply time spent in the presence of God celebrating *who* He is, *what* He has done, and *where* He is leading you. Praise builds up your relationship with God and helps put you in a place where the anointing of the Spirit of God can operate in your life.

When the Lord began to deal with me about writing this book, He began to show me that there was an incredible blessing upon the life of Boaz. Boaz lived a life of abundance. He was in a place of praise. Because of where he was and the favor that was upon his life, he had overflow more than what he needed or could use. Boaz even prospered in spite of the famine. His barns were full. He was able to give out of his overflow. That's the kind of favor God wants His people to be able to walk in, and it begins by pursuing the presence of God through praise.

In order to get herself in a position to partake in the blessing of Boaz, Naomi had to pursue praise. Remember this—your pursuit of praise will lead you out of Moab. It will lead you to the place where God's blessings can flow freely into your life.

Naomi had heard that God was supplying food for the people of Judah. Upon hearing that word of hope, she decided to return home. She was not expecting great blessings upon her arrival, she was just hoping for survival. But that seed of hope served to produce enough faith in her to step out from the boundaries of her bondage onto the road that would lead to her freedom. She was not really expecting favor to be waiting for her. She was not expecting an inheritance to be stored up for her. She had no idea that several thousand years later, people would still be talking about her and the impact she had on the world.

See, when you chase after praise; when you pursue the heart of God—you will *always* impact the lives of others. Your determination to go after God will sweep people into the Kingdom of God.

Naomi's determination to get out of her Moab Moment and go back to the place where God is exalted and glorified is what made it easy for Ruth to partner with her in that journey. We'll talk more about Ruth's decision later, but it was Naomi's initial step toward praise that drew Ruth into relationship with God and that caused the release of Boaz's blessing to come into their lives.

In Moab, you will not feel very blessed or favored. You will not feel very powerful, successful, or joyful. You will feel miserable, down, discouraged, frustrated, angry, and all the other emotions that come with being in a difficult place. What you have to keep in mind during these seasons is this—Moab Moments do not have the final say in your life. They do not have the final authority. If you will point your face toward Judah and pursue the presence of God, you will have full access to all that is in the Father's storehouse.

Moab has claimed its share of victims. You can die in Moab and be a victim, or you can take the pathway of praise and leave Moab behind. It is a choice that we as believers must make. See, just because you are in Moab does not mean you are not saved, it just means you are not experiencing God's optimum for your life. When you find yourself in a Moab Moment, the key is to limit the amount of time there as much as possible. Don't pitch a tent there and put down roots, get out! Get to a place where God's blessings can flow freely into your life.

THE DECISION DILEMMA

There is no substitute for being able to process the information at hand and make a quality decision that has a positive outcome. Life's dilemmas often do not come with instructions on how to overcome them. We are often faced with trying to make decisions that will have a major impact on both our future and the future of those who depend on us.

The decisions we make will often stay with us for a lifetime. Where to go to college, what profession to pursue, who to marry, how many children to have, where to live, where to go to church—these are just some of the major choices we all face.

There was a song I sang as a child that said, "I have decided to follow Jesus, no turning back, no turning back." Other verses to the song started with the declaration, "Tho none go with me, still I will follow…", "the cross before me, the world behind me…", "take this whole world, but give me Jesus…" and perhaps there were others ("I Have Decided to Follow Jesus" by S. Sundar Singh-public domain). Each verse was a declaration of the decision of that songwriter to follow Jesus, come what may. While some decisions in life may be harder to make, our decision to follow Christ must be one upon which all other decisions flow out of.

Every one of us has had the joy of making quality decisions and we have also had the misfortune of having made decisions that did not work out so well. As a pastor and a leader for over thirty years now, I can assure you that decisions I have made have blessed some and injured others. Such is the life of a leader. As a leader, one cannot be gun shy about making decisions. However, we must be willing to live with and accept the outcome of the decisions we make.

I remember many years ago during my freshman year of college that I was invited to attend the band fraternity's *ice cream social*. Now, understand, I had been raised in a pastor's home and came to the college life from a very small town of less than five thousand people in rural West Texas. When we offered someone ice cream, we meant ice cream, not beer.

I had never tasted beer. I had never wanted to taste beer. The smell was enough to kill that temptation in my life. But now I was away at school and my parents were not there to see my every move. I was making my own decisions.

We were instructed to come to a certain location with a bowl and a spoon and the ice cream would be there. I was the only dummy that showed up with a bowl and a spoon. Everyone else knew somehow that there was no ice cream involved. I never felt so humiliated in all my life. They showed me where the beer was and told me to get all I wanted.

Right then I had to make a decision—what was I going to? Would I make a decision that could potentially set me on a path of destruction, or would I choose to do what was right? This was actually one of the times I made the right decision and asked for a coke.

The decisions we make will lead us into bondage, keep us in bondage, or set us free from bondage. We must consider carefully our decisions, because they will either lead us into our destiny or keep us from reaching our destiny.

There are three key decisions made in the first chapter of Ruth. The first was when Naomi determined to return to Judah. The next was when Orpah chose not to go to Judah, and the final decision was when Ruth opted to stay with Naomi.

Naomi's decision to leave Moab was vital to her survival. She knew that if she remained where she was, she was for all intents and purposes choosing death; waving the white flag of surrender and giving up.

Had there been no one to consider but herself, who knows how she would have responded, but her decision to stay or to go also affected the lives of her two daughters-in-law, Orpah and Ruth. They were a family. Moab was Ruth and Orpah's homeland. They had been born there, grown up there, and knew nothing else but life in that kind of environment. In spite of that, when Naomi told them of her decision to go back to Judah, they began the journey with her.

Along the way Naomi began thinking about what her son's wives were doing. These two young ladies were leaving their homeland, friends, and family. They were departing from the life they knew and were accustomed to, leaving established relationships and traditions behind.

No doubt, she was also concerned about how she was going to provide for these two women. She encouraged them to return to the home of their mothers. She felt that by returning to Moab they could find another husband and be cared for. It is at this point that the burden of the decision whether or not to pursue praise (remember Judah means praise) switches from the shoulders of Naomi to the shoulders of Ruth and Orpah. Now they had to decide for themselves what path they were going to take.

Perhaps the choice of freedom is not an easy choice when freedom has never been seen, felt, or experienced. Perhaps the decision to enter into a place of praise, provision, and purpose is hard to make when one has nothing with which to compare those things. If all one has ever known is struggle, hardship, and lack; the promise of more often seems like an impossible obstacle to overcome, hence they choose to stay in Moab because they feel as though they do not deserve anything more.

Hear me—it's not about what you deserve or do not deserve. It's about what the Father has in store for you. It's about what He desires to give you, and you will never have those things in Moab.

After much persuasion, Orpah decided to go back to Moab. Had she been able to really understand what was awaiting her in Judah she could have shared in the same blessings that Naomi and Ruth would soon enjoy, but she chose to go back.

There is a strong spiritual principle here—freedom is never found in retreat but rather in the pressing forward beyond the barriers. Breakthrough will only be discovered as one presses through their present set of circumstances. Refuse to go back. All you will get when you go back is the same thing you had before you left. If it did not bless you then, it will not bless you now.

Ruth on the other hand made a clean break with her past. She forsook her old life completely. She asked Naomi not to encourage her to go back. Her mind was made up. She even told Naomi, "Where you go I will go, and where you lodge I will lodge. Your people will be my people and your God my God. Where you die I will die, and there will I be buried." This was a key decision in her partaking of the blessing to come. Her decision to forsake her old life and embrace the life God had for her produced powerful results in her life.

That decision set the course for their lives. It caused Naomi to be reassured that returning to Judah was the right thing to do.

Basically Ruth was telling her, "I don't care what kind of life I had in Moab. I don't care what kind of relationships

I had in Moab. I am linked to you, Naomi. I am joined to you. I am committed to you and to your journey. I will not stop half way. I will not fail to complete the journey. I will run the race set before me and I will run it well. I will not be deterred, nor will I be dissuaded. I have made my decision, I have set my face like a flint, and I am going all the way to the finish line with you."

We find a similar occurrence in the lives of Elijah and Elisha. We find their story in Second Kings. Elijah found Elisha plowing behind a yoke of oxen on his parent's farm and after touching him with his mantle, took him under his wing to prepare him to take over his ministry. After much travel they found themselves at Gilgal. As they were leaving Gilgal to go to Bethel, Elijah encouraged Elisha to stay behind. Elisha refused. Again at Bethel Elijah encouraged him to stay behind, and again Elisha refused. At Jericho Elisha one more time refused to stay behind. As he was preparing to cross Jordan and be caught away, Elijah tried one more time to get Elisha to stay behind, and one more time he refused.

There were fifty students from Elijah's school who refused to make the journey with them, but Elisha wanted the anointing that was on Elijah. Upon seeing his persistence, Elijah asked Elisha what he could do for him before he was to be taken away. Elisha asked for a double portion. Elijah told him, "If you see me when I leave, you can have what you ask for." That's exactly what happened. A chariot from heaven came and Elisha saw Elijah leave. The double portion of Elijah's anointing was his.

Had he not made the decision to leave his parents life of farming behind; had he stayed in Gilgal, Bethel, Jericho, or on the wrong side of Jordan, the double portion would have never been extended to him. But because of his decision to go all the way with Elijah, he was able to ask for and receive the anointing that God wanted to give him. That anointing was his harvest for the seed he had sown by investing his life in the life of Elijah.

There will always be a harvest when you make good decisions. There will always be a provision and a harvest when you purpose to pursue God. While there will always be others with more than you have and some with less than you have, you will have your need met and supplied out of God's storehouse because you have chosen to walk in obedience to His Word in your life.

It is important to insert right here that just because you choose to do right does not mean the road will be an easy one. It is not free from hardship, struggle, or opposition. When Ruth and Naomi arrived in Bethlehem scripture tells us that the whole town was in an uproar at Naomi's return. The King James Version says the town was *moved* at their return. The Amplified says the town was *stirred*. The Hebrew for this verse gave the understanding that not everyone was pleased that she had come home and brought this foreigner with her. Their right decision caused an uproar even in the place where praise was practiced.

In Ruth 1:20-21 we gain some insight as to Naomi's frame of mind when she arrived back in Bethlehem. She asked people not to call her by her name which means *pleasant*. She felt like the Lord had punished her for going to Moab. She asked to be called Mara which means *bitter*. Then she makes this statement, "I went out full, but the Lord has brought me home again empty."

I can't tell you the number of lives I have witnessed through the years that share that testimony. They were in a good place, and because of the circumstances of life made a decision to go to Moab. When they saw that Moab was not their answer and they wanted to come back home, they always came home empty.

Remember the story of the prodigal? He left his father's house full. He left blessed. He left with his pockets full. But when he came home, he came home empty. Oh, but the good part is that because of his decision to go back to his father's house, there was a harvest waiting for him. "Kill the fatted calf, put a robe on him and place a ring in his finger, and place shoes on his feet for my son that was lost is found." (author's paraphrase - Luke 15:23-24). What a harvest!

The very last statement of chapter one is perhaps the most powerful. "And they came to Bethlehem at the beginning of the barley harvest." (Ruth 1:22 KJV). God had already provided a time and a season of harvest to coincide with their return to Judah! They entered Judah expecting nothing, wondering how they were going to survive, and all the while God had prepared a harvest for them to partake in.

You need to know that if you are pursuing God with all that is within you, there is a harvest that is coming your way. It may not come all at one time. It most likely will not, but it will come. It will be there when you need it. God's supply will be there to sustain and see you through. Your day of harvest will come my friend. Do not doubt, but believe that it is on its way. Expect it. Confess it. Believe it. God gets no glory in your failure, but stands ready to pour into your life when you make the right decisions as we walk through life's dilemmas.

DIVINE FAVOR

I must admit I am guilty. I was that person in class, back in my school days, that was accused at times of being the teacher's pet. I was fortunate enough to figure out early in school that if I was courteous to the teacher, the dividends were wonderful. It would be fair to say that because of the choice I made to treat my teachers with dignity and respect, that I was granted favor in the classroom. Certain favor is earned, and there is such a thing as *divine favor* or *uncommon favor* that is given to you just because you have captured the heart of God.

Scripture records that David was a man *after God's own heart*. His passion and purpose was to pursue the very heart and nature of God the Father. He wanted to please God in all that he did. Because of that, he was granted incredible victories and was able to kill the enemies that pursued him. The bottom line is this: the choices you make will help to position you to be blessed by God. When you choose Him and His commandments; when you seek to do His will and live a life that pleases Him, you have positioned yourself for His favor to be upon you.

Now, let's define the word *favor*. Favor simply means *unearned privilege or blessing*. It means *unfair partiality, to prefer unfairly*. Someone said, "Favor is not fair." While it is true that God is no respecter of persons, some fail to walk in favor because of disobedience in their lives.

What I hope to do in this chapter is to teach you a little about how to position yourself to walk under the hand of God's incredible favor. There are some powerful principles that when followed will bring God's favor on your life. These are not in any particular order of importance, but they are the things that will change your life when embraced.

The first principle that must be mentioned is the *principle of sowing and reaping*. I am fully aware that this subject has been addressed by much more studied minds than mine, but it is such a huge key in the life of Boaz that it simply cannot be overlooked.

Boaz was a farmer, so he understood the principle of sowing and reaping on a very natural level. Where there is no sowing, there is no watering, no fertilizing or nurturing of the crop, then there's no harvesting of the crop. And since there is no harvest, there are no barns, no supply, no reserve, no abundance, and no ability to meet your need, much less the needs of others.

Second Corinthians 9:10 (KJV) says, "Now He who supplies seed to the sower and bread for food will also supply and increase your store of seed and enlarge the harvest of your righteousness."

Boaz understood that the seed for future sowing would be contained within the harvest he was reaping. Harvest is *not* just about eating. It is about seed for the next crop and the storage of seed to give to others so they can have seed to sow.

This sound so elementary but so many in the body of Christ have failed to grasp this most basic principle. *There is no harvest unless you sow.* It really is that simple. And the sad thing is, there are scores of angry, hurt, bitter people running around accusing the church of just being *money hungry* when they talk about tithing or the giving of offerings.

I can tell you, and God is my witness, I have preached and taught numerous times on the subject of giving, and never has my motive been to get. My motive has always been the hope that people would understand and grasp this powerful principle in their lives, so they would be delivered from lack and walk in God's favor.

I have yet to understand the thought that without an investment there is somehow a reward. Even the gift of salvation, or the *harvest* of salvation, comes with the investment of your faith to believe that Jesus is the Son of God and that He paid the price on the cross for your sins. By far, the vast majority of people who have sat in my office over the years needing the church to assist them financially are people who do not tithe, do not give offerings, and people who are not submitted to spiritual authority. They spend their seed on the profane and unholy and get upset at the church for not feeding them. The reason they are in lack is because they have failed to understand that until they begin to plant, they will always be in lack.

Even in famine, Boaz prospered. Why? Because he already had seed stored to sow from his last harvest. Because he had sown, he had abundance. It was out of his overflow that he was able to bless those around him. His sowing provided, *not only* for his family, but it also provided employment for others doing the harvesting. It provided food for the gleaners. It fed those who could not feed themselves. Out of his overflow, the needs of the widows and orphans were met. Had he not sown, famine would have destroyed him.

Tithing and the giving of offerings is not about the pastor having a better car or a bigger house—although there are a lot of pastors who could use such blessing. It's about there being something in the storehouse so that when famines come, there is enough in the barn to sustain the body. It is about the release of God's favor in the lives of God's people knowing that as they give and as they release what is in their hand, God in turn releases what is in his.

I remember a statement I heard years ago that said, "God may not need your money, but you need His harvest." This principle worked for Boaz, and it is still working today.

This principle not only worked in the life of Boaz, but we discover it in the life of Ruth as well. She had bound herself to Naomi, to her people, and to her God. She had left the place of her birth to discover the place of her blessing. She had nothing to sow but herself and her time.

As she was gleaning the fields of Boaz, he noticed her and began to inquire about her. He was impressed by her willingness to be a blessing to Naomi, and he began to order his servants to bless her.

In Ruth 2:10 (NIV), we find Ruth asking an interesting question of Boaz. "Why have I found favor in your eyes that you should notice me, when I am a foreigner?" In other words, "I have come into your land, into your field having nothing to offer, yet you have shown me kindness and offered me grace. What makes you do that for me?"

That is how we were when Jesus found us. We were strangers with nothing but our lives to give, and he accepted that and showered upon us His goodness and His grace. He showed us love before we knew of his love. He took us like we were so He could begin the process of making us into what He knows we can become. Because she was willing to sow her life, the blessing of Boaz—or one could say the favor of the father— began to be released into her life and was bestowed upon her.

The second principle I want to look at is the *principle of influence*. Now remember, we are talking about divine or uncommon favor. Favor will earn you influence, and influence will earn you favor; but influence comes through relationship. In fact, favor comes through relationship!

What is influence? According to *Webster's Dictionary*, "Influence is the act or power of producing an effect without apparent exertion of force or direct exercise of command." Influence is often held by persons of high social or economic standing and/or persons in positions of authority.

One of the greatest Biblical stories of influence to me is the story of Nehemiah. While it is true that he was a man of wealth and position; he was also a man of relationship. He was properly positioned to receive uncommon favor. He was the king's cupbearer. He was with the king on a daily basis. He served the king faithfully. His relationship and his faithfulness *earned* him influence with the king and because of that influence, he received the favor of the king to go and rebuild the walls of Jerusalem. And not just rebuild, but the favor extended to the provision for materials as well.

The favor of God on your life will give you influence in your city. A pastor especially needs to know that. As long as they never see outside the four walls of their church, they will never have an affect on the city nor be effective in the city. The need for influence is great in the church today. The world has seen our ugly side, our human side, our faults and our failures. It's time they see the presence of the Lord in us and on us. It's time they see Jesus reflected in all we do. When we learn to *be* the church and not just learn how to *do* church, we will influence the world to go in the direction God is leading.

Look back at the definition of influence. Influence is power. Boaz used his power as an employer and land owner to protect Ruth and to make sure she was cared for. The indication is given in chapter two that rape and molestation of the young ladies who gleaned was a major problem. Boaz used his influence to command the young men not to touch Ruth. Boaz even told Ruth that the young men would draw fresh water for her anytime she grew thirsty. He used his influence to pour favor upon her.

Boaz had the power to send Ruth away. He could have looked the other way while the young men in the field had their way with her. He could have chosen not to allow her to glean in the fields. He could have chosen not to leave handfuls on purpose for her to gather, but because he knew what it was to walk in favor, he extended his favor upon her.

We see in chapter four that Boaz also had influence with the city leaders. He sat in the gate of the city and had enough influence to gather ten of the city's elders together to discuss the redemption of Ruth. He had enough influence to lead that discussion. His character, his integrity, and his willingness to stay the course during the season of famine earned him the right to be heard in the gates of the city. If you will stay on the course that God has set before you, and run that race with patience you will find that uncommon favor will be upon you as you seek to follow God.

The *third area of favor* I want to present is the *favor of birthright*. The word birthright means the rights that a person has because he was born in a certain family, nation, etc. It also means the rights of the firstborn (heritage).

Birthrights were blessing bestowed upon the son from the father. The reason Boaz had what he had is because his father before him passed land to him as an inheritance. In those days everything was passed down from generation to generation. Those who were good managers and good stewards could become very wealthy and powerful. No doubt Boaz was in such a position.

Ruth had no birthright. She had no inheritance. Apart from favor she would have lived her life in obscurity. It's amazing how God can take the foolish things and confound the wise, the base things and transform them into something mighty and powerful. We see it over and over again in scripture how God has taken people who by the world's standards should not have been qualified, but God used them to be world shakers. Even though they may not have been born into the right family to receive a natural inheritance, they were *grafted in* or adopted by God into His family, and there favor found them. There they discovered they have a birthright. There they discovered they are of royal birth. There they discovered they are of royal blood.

The favor of the birthright is the favor of family. You are not some lone ranger out there fighting for truth and justice all on your own. You are connected to the family of God. When you get connected to the family of God, get connected to a local church, and get connected to people who can encourage you in your relationship with God, you begin to discover the favor that comes with being a part of God's great family.

Boaz gave Ruth what she did not have—a family who could give her an inheritance—plus he put her in the position to pass that inheritance on to future generations. Boaz gave her the opportunity to not just be a partaker in his heritage but to be a partaker in his legacy.

There are so many things that could be touched on as we talk about divine favor, but allow me just one more area that when we have it operating in our lives will position us for great favor. I will call this one the *favor of longevity*.

There are three words that come to mind when I think of longevity. They are loyalty, faithfulness, and planted. We are living in a day and age when these words have lost their meaning both in the church and out of the church. If the church is going to have the impact it needs to have in the world today, we must rediscover and reapply these elements in our lives.

My grandfather on my father's side was born in North Carolina in 1904, just down the road a bit from where that same year the Wright Brothers flew their first plane. All through the depression he and my grandmother did better than most. They were blessed to be able to provide for their family even in hard times. As I grew older, I saw something in his life that taught me one of the secrets to success. Longevity, loyalty, faithfulness, and the ability to get planted.

I was born in 1960 but remember vividly going to my grandfather's retirement party in the mid-sixties. As a young boy of five or six, it meant nothing to me at the time, but as a grown man and a grandfather myself now, it means a lot to me. He worked for the same company, Southwestern Bell Telephone for forty-four years. That is unthinkable today. One job for forty-four years. He sang in the same church choir at the same church for forty years. Yes, you heard me, forty years in one church. He did not jump the fence every time something happened he did not like. He stayed put. He was more proud of those forty years in the choir than he was his forty-four years at the phone company. He knew the value of being planted.

As he neared the end of his life I drove out to West Texas to see him one final time before he died. His health had declined to such a level that he depended on others to help him with the normal functions of life. I was putting him back in the car and telling him goodbye knowing that I would most likely never see him alive again, then he looked up at me and said, "Bruce, whatever you do, don't ever give up. Don't ever give up. If you give up, it's over." There has been countless times in my life when his final words to me have been what have helped me put one foot in front of the other and continue my journey.

Today people change jobs, change spouses, swap families, change churches, and change friends at the drop of a hat. Psalm 1 tells us that blessings come to the one who is *planted by the rivers of living water.* Something that is planted in good soil is not easily uprooted. Too many in the body of Christ today are like these plants you purchase at a nursery; they are planted, but only in pots, not in the ground. You will never take root and produce fruit until you get planted in good soil and put down roots.

One of the reasons Boaz had such incredible favor in Judah is because he had become planted there. He put down roots. He was determined to stay the course regardless of the storm. It's easy to leave in a storm. It's easy to leave when others are leaving. It's easy to leave when it looks like the harvest is going to fail, or when the silo appears to be running out of grain, but I contend that if we are faithful to the call, faithful to the vision, faithful to the Word of God, and faithful to the will of God we will eat in times of famine, our vats will overflow with wine and oil, and the harvest will be more than enough!

I can tell you from personal experience that staying put during difficult times is not the easiest thing to do. It is always easier to quit than it is to fight. It is always easier to run away than it is to take a stand. But the armor of God is provided to us for warfare. It covers us so we can advance, not retreat. The Body of Christ *must* get back to a place where we know what it means to put down roots and teach by our lives the model of faithfulness.

The root word of faithfulness is faith. One cannot be found faithful apart from having faith. The exercise of faith is required for longevity to be realized. You have to have faith in what God has called you to, faith in the direction He has called you to walk, faith in those God has placed around you, faith in your spiritual authority and leadership, faith in God's ability to see you through both the good times as well as the trying times.

James 1 teaches us that when we ask of God, we should ask in faith "nothing wavering. He that wavers is like a wave of the sea driven with the wind and tossed." The next two verses say that the one who asks with wavering faith will receive nothing because that person is unstable in all that they do.

This instability will keep you from advancing. It will keep you from operating in the favor God has for you. The divine favor of God will never fall upon the unstable. It is those who operate in a faith that believes beyond a doubt that God is who he says he is and He can do what he says he can do; those are the ones who will find favor flowing in their lives.

Here is the summation. You can position yourself to be blessed and to walk in the favor of God. It is not something that is given only to a select few. Favor is for family. It comes from the Father. It is there not just to meet your needs but to provide increase. So position yourself by doing the things that please the Father. Make Him proud of you! If it worked for Boaz, it will work for you. The principles of God are timeless.

THE COVENANT CONNECTION

The word *covenant* is one which is seldom used today but is one that is vital we understand if you want to walk in the blessings God has for your life. The ability to keep a covenant is crucial to any successful relationship. When covenants are broken, relationships fail.

One of the foundational stones in a covenant is trust, or if you prefer, faith. Problems arise when we began to make covenants with those with whom no trust has been established. Covenants are not something we should enter into lightly, and they should only be made after much prayer. But trust in the one with whom the covenant is being made will produce strength and longevity with that covenant.

Now, let's define what a covenant is. According to *Webster's Dictionary*, "A covenant is a binding and solemn agreement made by two or more individuals, parties, etc to do or keep from doing a specified thing—a compact or contract."

A covenant binds two things together. It is a promise that is agreed upon by those who enter the covenant and the parties are willing to sign their name to the promise.

After the flood of Noah, God made a covenant vow that He would never again destroy man in that fashion, and he sealed that vow by placing a rainbow in the sky. In the New

Testament God sent Jesus to redeem us from sin's curse. He made a covenant with man—if we would apply the blood of Christ to our lives we would have eternal life. That covenant is still in force today.

The most visible model of a covenant relationship is a marriage. The two parties agree to love each other regardless of the obstacles until they are separated by death. It is meant to be a lifelong agreement. When the vows get broken, the love is destroyed, and the marriage crumbles.

Let me just insert this right here. I cannot over emphasize the importance of being cautious on *what* and *who* you covenant with. The Word issues the warning not to be unequally yoked with unbelievers. You have to be careful in business who you partner with just as you do in your marriage relationship. You cannot start off on a less than secure foundation and hope it will get better over time. If the foundation is not strong; if those entering the covenant are not equal in their trust and faith, the relationship will likely not stand when times of testing come.

Boaz was a man who understood covenant. He had witnessed the incredible relationship between his mother and his father. He grew to understand that covenant includes acceptance, mercy, grace, forgiveness, and it provides a covering for the one with whom we come in covenant with. It was these traits that became a part of his life and later his covenant with Ruth.

I want to look at three aspects of a covenant in this chapter. First we will look at *the purpose of covenant.*

When I first began this journey into the Book of Ruth and the study of Boaz, a phrase came into my spirit that I believe is appropriate right here. The phrase is this, "The company you keep will affect your destiny." If you want to go the distance in your destiny you have to surround yourself with the right people. The purpose of covenant is to help you reach your destiny, not just go on a trip.

The first question that must be asked when one enters a covenant is—why? Why do I want to covenant with this person, or this business, or this church? Why does this person want to covenant with me? Our motive must be pure so the purpose can be achieved.

Here are some of the purposes for establishing a covenant:

> it provides accountability;
> gives you someone or something to invest your life in;
> creates a strategic partnership;
> elevates your level of effectiveness;
> increases your resources; and
> to bind two parts together to form a whole

All of these things are evident in the story of Ruth and Boaz. Ruth established a covenant with Naomi when she refused to return to Moab. She even put her voice to it when she declared, "Your people will be my people and your God will be my God." She was binding herself to Naomi.

She was cutting all ties with her past and binding herself to someone to whom she was willing to entrust her future.

Isn't that what the Apostle Paul instructed us to do in Philippians 3:13-15? Let me remind you what it says,

> "[13]I do not consider, brethren, that I have captured and made it my own [yet]; but one thing I do [it is my one aspiration]: forgetting what lies behind and straining forward to what lies ahead,
>
> [14]I press on toward the goal to win the [supreme and heavenly] prize to which God in Christ Jesus is calling us upward.
>
> [15]So let those [of us] who are spiritually mature and full-grown have this mind and hold these convictions; and if in any respect you have a different attitude of mind, God will make that clear to you also. (AMP)"

Ruth was willing to forget and forsake her past so she could forge ahead. Covenant will help you break off what needs to be broken off and will help you bind with what needs to be bonded to. Part of the purpose of covenant is to forget and forsake. Covenant requires a refraining from as well as an adhering to.

Another purpose of covenant is to bring about a change. When you covenant with the right people and the right things, it produces change in your life. You can begin to walk in an expectancy that your life will be blessed, not cursed. You can walk in the expectancy that you'll walk in health and not sickness, and so on. When you bind yourself to something or someone that is *already* being blessed, you receive part of that blessing.

It's like joining a church. I teach people that in order to be fruitful and to have a positive experience in the local church; you have to get planted there. Find a place where the Spirit of God is free to move, a place where freedom dwells, a place where there is life, love, and unity—and get planted. *That* is a covenant. When you join, you are forming a covenant with that pastor and that body. You are committing your energy, your efforts, your wisdom, your resources, your talents, your gifts to the fulfilling of the vision of that house. And because that House is blessed, you can expect to be blessed as well.

In the case of Ruth and Naomi, Naomi was blessed and did not even know it. She had an inheritance and did not realize it. There was provision for her in Judah that she knew not of. See, when we come into covenant with God, there is blessing, inheritance, and provision that was waiting on us all the time…God was just waiting for us to find our created purpose which is serve God with all our heart, mind, body, and soul.

Now let us look at the *power of covenant.*

A covenant by its definition denotes strength. There is a force with it and because of it. It is no longer the power of one, but the power of at least two. No one can do alone what two can do as a team. A true covenant typifies teamwork.

Each party brings their strengths and abilities to the table and as they join forces, great power can be realized.

We have witnessed that in the business world over the years. Verizon purchased Alltel making them the largest cell phone company in America. Both businesses were successful. Both had large markets. Both had successful advertising campaigns. But as they merged and became one…they generated a much larger market share, a larger revenue pool, and more potential customers.

I want us to take a look at three examples from scripture that demonstrate the power of covenant.

The first is the familiar story of the three Hebrew children. Shadrach, Meshach and Abednego were three very courageous teens who loved God with a passion. They were bound to Him. They honored him and understand what covenant was. They did not take serving God lightly, to them it was all or nothing.

They were not willing to void that covenant regardless of the payoff or the consequences. The King had made some harsh demands. He had ordered people's allegiance and their worship to be upon an image made by man rather than upon God. Their worship was not for sale nor for barter. Their relationship with God was not up for negotiation. They were bound to a higher power and higher authority than the King and they were convinced that the power of their covenant would be more than enough to protect them from any consequences the King could dish out. So they refused the King's decree and stood firm in their covenant with God.

Here is the power of standing in a covenant that is right. Not only were they unaffected by the heat of the furnace, not only were the ropes that bound them burned away, but Jesus came and walked with them in the fire. Covenant with God produces spiritual power. Jesus will walk with those who covenant with Him. He will not leave them nor will He forsake them. He will not leave them in times of difficulty, but will walk with them through that time of hardship and show them the way out.

Now, here's the rest of the story. The power of that covenant not only produced the presence of God, it changed the atmosphere of the Kingdom and it changed the heart of the King to the place where he issued a *new* decree that the God of Shadrach, Meshach and Abednego was the *real* God, and he is the only one that would be served in that kingdom!

What a change! All because of covenant!

The second story is one of my personal favorites in all of scripture, and that is the story of the prodigal son. He had a covenant with his father by virtue of birth. Now the father was better at keeping the covenant than the son was. The son was impulsive, inquisitive, immature, and impetuous. He wanted to see the world and he was willing to both break fellowship with his father, and sacrifice his future in order to experience what the world had to offer.

He had never known life outside of his father's house. But the lure was too great, so he asked for his share of the birthright and left home. He spent his money foolishly to the point of going broke. He wound up in a hog pen feeding the hogs and craving the food he gave to them.

It's amazing how when our idea does not work we want to remember how good the father's way was. The Bible says the son *came to himself* and realized that even those who worked the fields and served at his father's house had life better than he had it, so he decided to go home and ask to be a servant.

Now remember—covenant says, "I will regardless of what you do." As far as the father was concerned, the covenant was still intact. He had spent his days going out to the road longing to see the face of his son, hoping to see him returning home. The power of the covenant was still strong in his life and still very active.

One day, the father went out the road like he had done countless times before. I don't believe really that he expected today to be any different, but his prayer was no doubt the same. He wanted the safe return of his son.

As he peered down the road, he saw a figure approaching. No one had to tell the father who it was. No one had to encourage him to go and greet his son. The Bible tells us that he saw the son *afar off* and he ran to him, kissed him, and welcomed him home.

The power of the covenant is that he was not forced to live as a servant, but was given his place back as a son. In addition, a celebration was held in his honor because the lost son had returned home.

The power of covenant is restoration and recovery. When you get the covenant relationship right, you can expect restoration and recovery. Because the father was willing to keep the covenant in force, the son was able to be restored.

I have touched on this but let me say it another way. It is perceived that a covenant would be 50/50, but in reality it is 100/100. Both sides have to give 100 percent of themselves to the partnership. That's called *unity*. Yes, the son failed to give his percentage, but the father was still 100 percent committed and that's what laid the foundation for restoration.

The lesson here is this—if you have broken covenant, repent and get back in covenant. If someone has broken covenant with you, offer forgiveness and make room for restoration and recovery in their lives.

The third example of the power of covenant is found in the life of David. Saul was King at the time and he and David were at war with one another. Saul was trying to kill David. But David and Saul's son, Jonathan were very close friends. Jonathan came to David and told him that Saul would not kill him, and that he would one day rule as king over Israel. Then the Bible tells us that they made a covenant together before the Lord. They had made a covenant before that time. Jonathan took his robe and gave it to David. He gave him his sword and his bow as well as a sign of that covenant.

Now this may not seem like a big deal until years later. Saul was dead and David was King. Jonathan was dead, and most of Saul's other next of kin is also dead. David began to inquire if there are any descendants remaining from the house of Saul. Someone told him of a son that Jonathan had named Mephibosheth. David came to learn that Mephibosheth had suffered a fall when he was only five years old and was crippled in both legs. He lived in a place called Lodebar.

Here he was the grandson of the previous King and the son of the former prince. Life used to be good. At one time he was welcome at the palace. At one time he had privilege, but all that was gone now, and here he was crippled from a fall living in Lodebar. When you look up Lodebar in the Hebrew it means *a place of desolation where no life dwells.* It was a dry, barren, meager existence. No trees, grass, or vegetation could grow easily there.

David sends for him and tells him in 2 Samuel 9:7-13: (NIV)

> "Don't be afraid," David said to him, "for I will surely show you kindness for the sake of your father Jonathan.
> I will restore to you all the land that belonged to your grandfather Saul, and you will always eat at my table."

Mephibosheth bowed down and said, "What is your servant, that you should notice a dead dog like me?"

Then the king summoned Ziba, Saul's servant, and said to him, "I have given your master's grandson everything that belonged to Saul and his family. You and your sons and your servants are to farm the land for him and bring in the crops, so that your master's grandson may be provided for. And Mephibosheth, grandson of your master, will always eat at my table." Now Ziba had fifteen sons and twenty servants.

Then Ziba said to the king, "Your servant will do whatever my lord the king commands his servant to do." So Mephibosheth ate at David's table like one of the king's sons.

Mephibosheth had a young son named Mica, and all the members of Ziba's household were servants of Mephibosheth. And Mephibosheth lived in Jerusalem, because he always ate at the king's table, and he was crippled in both feet.

The reason David did this was because of the covenant he had made with Jonathan many years before. The power of that covenant took a hopeless cripple and gave him hope. It gave him life. Where once he had no substance, he now ate at the King's table and had people to take care of him.

That's where Jesus found us. We were crippled from a fall. We lived in a dry, barren place and had no life, no hope, no real joy, and no peace. But the King had made a covenant with mankind that said if we would apply the blood of his son Jesus to our lives, we could eat from the King's table.

Let me tell you friend, covenant is a part of our life. We can't get around it. We can't get away from it. You can either walk in it and experience its power and be blessed by it, or you can avoid it and live in Lodebar.

I can assure you, life in the presence of the King is far better than life in Lodebar. Covenant will bring you out of your Lodebar and place you in the presence of the King!

Finally, let's look at the *potential of covenant.*

Every covenant has the potential of success or failure. Success depends on the level of commitment and energy people are willing to apply to the relationship. See, every relationship has the potential to produce covenant, but most do not, because we are unwilling or unable to make the commitment required for a successful covenant with more than just a few people.

There were plenty of opportunities for the covenant between Ruth and Naomi to fail. There were differences, hardships, roadblocks, obstacles, hurdles, barriers, not to mention the cultural differences. They were raised different, had a different concept of God, and had different life experiences, but covenant looked past all that and bound them together.

Covenant looks on the heart. It looks at one's motives. It finds the treasure in others and seeks to strengthen the other person. It looks past the disagreements, disappointments, miscommunications, and frustrations that come with relationship, and seeks to establish unity.

One of the greatest examples of the potential of covenant I find in scripture is found in 2 Chronicles 7:14. "If my people which are called by my name, will humble themselves and pray, and seek my face, and turn from their wicked ways, then will I hear from heaven, I will forgive their sin, and I will heal their land."

Covenant has *world-changing* potential. Who would have thought that when Salmon (Boaz's father) married Rahab that their descendants would alter the course of humanity? That single covenant of marriage produced a bloodline that produced Mary who was the mother of Jesus. No one could have foreseen the blessing of that bloodline or the potential of that bloodline, but because of covenant the world was changed.

Ask yourself—what kind of potential do my covenants have? I'm sure when the parents of George Washington married; they never imagined the potential of that covenant. When the parents of Billy Graham married I doubt they knew that their son would influence world leaders and pray for presidents.

The business world is full of examples of strong covenants that have grown to be major players in the US and world economy. Sears and Roebuck, Abercrombie and Fitch, A and W Root Beer, Baskin-Robbins, Ben and Jerry's, Barnes and Nobel, are just a few that took advantage of forming strong covenants to make their business strong.

Even television knew the value of strategic partnerships—Amos and Andy, Batman and Robin, Starsky and Hutch, Sherlock Holmes and Dr. Watson are just a few that come to mind. The truth is no one rises very far by themselves, it takes partnership with others in order to succeed.

Only God knows what potential your covenants will have, but they *do* have potential. If that potential is pursued with great zeal and wisdom, the covenants you form could well be the catalyst that produces change in the lives of many.

COVENANT OF REDEMPTION

There is an old hymn that says, "Redeemed how I love to proclaim it, redeemed by the blood of the Lamb. Redeemed through HIs infinite mercy, His child and forever I am. Redeemed, redeemed, redeemed by the blood of the Lamb. Redeemed, redeemed, HIs child and forever I am" ("Redeemed" by Fanny J. Crosby, music by William Kirkpatrick).

Redemption. What a word! What a thought! What a concept! What a joy to experience this incredible gift that Christ has offered to those who will receive it by accepting Him. God saw humanity at its worst, yet still offered full price to redeem us from fear, frustration & failure to a life of freedom!

Webster's Dictionary defines the word *redeem* to mean the following: to buy back, to get back, to recover by paying a fee, to pay off, to set free, a ransom, to deliver from sin and its penalties as by a sacrifice made for the sinner, and to atone or compensate for.

Not only have we been redeemed from sin, but as well as from the *penalties* of sin. Those sins have been paid off and fully compensated for. No other price has to be paid for our redemption, Jesus paid it all.

When we accept that act of redemption, it is the formation of a covenant relationship with God. It could be said that redemption is a covenant. It is a holy covenant. For the potential of that covenant to be found, our relationship with God must grow. As we pursue the heart of God, He begins to unfold His vision, His plans, and His purpose for our lives and for our covenant together. As we walk in His will, we find He will be there to help, undergird, offer counsel, and lead the way.

One of the great stories of redemption in the Bible is the story of Abraham and Isaac. God had told Abraham to sacrifice his son Isaac. Abraham had waited twenty-five years for Isaac to be born. He was one hundred years old at the time of his birth. You can imagine the difficulty of waiting twenty-five years for a promise to be fulfilled but how much harder to have the one who fulfilled the promise ask that you give that gift back as a sacrifice. Abraham obeyed even though he did not understand.

As they neared the place of sacrifice they discovered the performance of a savior in the form of a ram who was caught in a thicket by his horns. God spoke to Abraham to release Isaac and sacrifice the ram instead.

Abraham's covenant with God allowed Abraham to trust God completely. God redeemed Isaac with a ram and eventually established the same covenant with him that He had with Abraham.

In this chapter, we will look at four covenants that played a role in Boaz's ultimate redemption of Ruth.

COVENANT OF PARTNERSHIP

Ruth's redemptive process really began when she made the decision *not* to return to Moab. When she told Naomi, "don't ask me anymore to go back, I'm not going back;" she set in motion a chain of events that would propel her into her destiny.

On the road between Moab and Judah she made what one could call a *destiny decision*. She formed a covenant of *partnership* with Naomi. I know I keep going back to this point in the story, but the importance of that moment simply cannot be over emphasized. That moment, that instance, that split second in time not only changed her life, but it changed the life of Naomi, Boaz, and many future generations. Her decision to partner with the right person gave her a future and a hope that she would have never had with any other partnership. Had she formed a covenant with Orpah that day, she would have died in Moab.

We talked in the previous chapter about the importance of with whom or what you covenant with. When forming partnerships, here are some of the key things to look at:

- Partner with someone who is not willing to settle for the status quo, but who will make the necessary sacrifices in order to achieve the desired result.

- Partner with someone who knows where they are going.

- Partner with someone with whom you can agree and with whom you can come into unity.

- Partner with someone who wants their future to be better than their today.

- Partner with someone who has experience or who is learning to learn from your experience.

Ruth did all of these things when she formed her partnership with Naomi on the road that day. Naomi may not have fully known what life held for her in Judah or even how she would be received, but she was unwilling to live life in Moab where there was no hope of a future. She was willing to lay everything on the line to journey to Judah. She knew where she was going, her mind was made up, and she was filled with determination to make the trip.

I don't know the full extent of what kind of relationship Ruth and Naomi had, but I do believe that Ruth trusted and respected Naomi completely. I believe that trust and respect were the foundational stones in her being willing to have a covenant relationship with Naomi.

Look again at the covenant words Ruth spoke to Naomi, "Don't urge me to leave you or turn back from you. Where you go I will go, and where you stay I will stay. Your people will be my people and your God my God. Where you die I will die, and there I will be buried. May the Lord deal with me, be it ever so severely, if anything but death separates you and me." (Ruth 1:16-17 NIV)

Those are covenant words if any have ever been spoken. She left no doubt in the mind of Naomi the extent of her loyalty and the depth of her commitment to their partnership.

Partnership is part of the redemptive process. One cannot redeem themselves. If man could have redeemed himself we would not have needed Jesus. Redemption requires the help of someone with greater resources than you have. Naomi could covenant with her, but could not redeem her. Here is an important principle to know—your covenant may not be your salvation, or your redemption, but it may take you on a journey that will lead you to the right connection. Ruth's connection to Naomi is what led her to Boaz.

A partnership can bring restoration and recovery into your life when nothing else can. If you are in a place where the enemy has plundered your fields and stolen from you I encourage you to find people that you can partner with that can teach you, instruct you, counsel you, and help you rebuild, recover, and be restored. You'll discover that being with the right people changes the atmosphere around you which changes you and your way of thinking. You go from stinking thinking to believing God can do anything!

Some of you who are in business perhaps can testify that when you made Jesus your business partner with controlling interest, your business became profitable and successful. That does not mean you have not had ups and downs, it just means that the down times did not cause you to close the doors…God still made a way and provided.

The bottom line is this—you need people in your life, and people need you in their life. Ask God to put you with the right people. That includes the right people to fellowship with, to pray with, to minister with, to worship with, and to connect with. Those partnerships could put someone on the path of redemption as you let God lead and direct your life.

THE COVENANT OF PROVISION

Here is another important principle to know, when you form the right covenants, provision always follows. We talked in an earlier chapter about Ruth 1:22.that says, "So Naomi returned from Moab accompanied by Ruth the Moabitess, her daughter-in-law, arriving in Bethlehem as the barley harvest was beginning."

The fact that they arrived at the beginning of the harvest season was the first clue that provision was coming, but Ruth still needed mercy. She still needed an application of grace from someone who had a field from which she could glean.

Something that people who are learning to trust God through tithing soon discover is you will often glean before you reap a full harvest. If you are grateful for the opportunity to glean and will be faithful in the gleaning, you will get to the place where you will have a field of your own and be able to bless others who need what the reapers leave behind.

The Apostle Paul was one who understood provision. He knew what it was for God to meet his need. In writing to the Christians in Philippi, he encouraged them by telling them, "But my God shall supply all your need according to His riches in glory, by Christ Jesus." Phillipians 4:19 KJV I heard a teacher many years ago say that those last three words, *by Christ Jesus* meant, *not of debt*, but by grace.

Paul was letting them know that because they had a covenant relationship with God, every need they had would be supplied. Not because it was a debt God owed, but because through Jesus our debts have been canceled, the curse of poverty has been destroyed, and sin's dominion over us has been broken. Because of Jesus, now our needs *can* be supplied. They can be supplied supernaturally.

I will never forget when we found out we were expecting our third daughter; we were in the process of shopping for insurance, but had not yet purchased any. We had just accepted the pastorate of a small church and they were providing the insurance, but we were shopping for the best deal when we found out that our third daughter was on the way. At that time the church was small and the finances, although growing, were still not sufficient to pay for the doctor and the hospital.

We paid on the doctor as much as we could, but still owed almost three thousand dollars just three days before the deadline. I had a banker in the church and could have borrowed the money but was praying that we would not have to go that route. I was at my desk three days before the due date when a man walked into my office and put a three-thousand-dollar check on my desk and said God told him we needed the money. He had no idea of our situation. We were able to pay the doctor in full.

After Kaelie was born; the hospital bill was thirteen thousand dollars. That debt was supernaturally erased as well! I believe the reason for that is we were in the right place, at the right time, with the right people, doing the right thing. When you do that, provision will be there when you need it.

See, God obligated Himself to supply and provide. When you tithe, He Himself will open the windows of heaven and personally pour out blessings beyond your ability to receive. That is a covenant of provision.

Boaz made a covenant of provision with Ruth. He told her, "Don't go and glean in another field and don't go away from here…watch the field where the men are harvesting and follow along after the girls…and whenever you are thirsty, go and get a drink from the water jars the men have filled." Later he expanded the provision by telling his men…

Even if she gathers among the sheaves, don't embarrass her. Rather, pull out some stalks for her from the bundles and leave for her to pick up…"

When you have come from Moab with nothing and you find yourself with more than enough…that's a breakthrough! Here is what provision does for you—it offers you breakthrough and it gives you the opportunity to offer breakthrough to others.

I'll never forget what my younger brother said about wealth. He is a successful doctor and businessman in Dallas, Texas. "Wealth," he said, "is not about the gathering of money. It is about the freedom and the choices that it brings into your life." Instead of saying, "I'd love to go to Hawaii someday," wealth gives you the freedom to say, "I'm going to Hawaii today." It takes a hope and makes it a reality.

That is what provision does for you. It empowers you to make choices rather than live with what the circumstances dictate to you. Moab told Ruth she would be hungry, destitute, and live a life of hardship, but once she entered into Judah (praise), she found a covenant relationship that said, "I'll make sure you have what you need." What a difference a covenant makes.

THE COVENANT OF PASSION

Passion is a great word. It is an ingredient you all need in your life if you are to reach any level of success at all.

Passion is the fuel that drives you forward. It is your zest for life and your zeal for Christ. It's what wakes you up in the morning and motivates you during the day. Passion. Passion is what kept Noah busy for 120 years while building an ark. Passion is what drove David to speak up and step out against Goliath. Passion is what helped Paul keep going even though he had been shipwrecked, imprisoned, and beaten.

You can recognize a church with passionate people because they eagerly do things that promote excellence. They willingly involve themselves in ministry opportunities, and they go out of their way to help the church to grow.

As a pastor, when people come to me looking for a position, I am very hesitant to provide much ministry space for them, but when I find people who are passionate, and just want to serve, I look for ways to help them find a place of service and a way that will allow for their promotion.

The streets of our cities are filled with those who have lost their passion. They have had their dreams stepped on so many times they fill like there is no use in pursuing it any longer. They have allowed the circumstances of their life to dictate their passion. Passion should be dictating the circumstance of life, not the other way around.

Boaz was a man of great passion. He was passionate about his work, he was passionate about the ways of God, and he was passionate about those who worked for him. He did not rule from the house, he went out to the fields and rubbed elbows with the workers.

When he saw Ruth and heard about all she had done for Naomi, Boaz became passionate about making sure she was cared for and provided for. That passion was mixed with compassion which over a period of time produced in him the desire to redeem her. Remember, we are still talking about the process of redemption.

In those days, when a man died and left a widow the next of kin had the right to purchase his property. However, when you purchased the property, the widow came with it and she was your responsibility to take care of and provide for. She would literally become your wife. Understand the custom of that day was for men to have many wives.

Boaz, knowing this, also knew that there was another kinsman who had the right of redemption before he did. So Boaz called a meeting with ten of the city elders and with the other relative to discuss the matter. Boaz offered the right of redemption to his relative, but upon realizing with the redemption, came the obligation of Naomi and Ruth, he declined. Boaz then put forth his covenant of redemption that sprang from the passion he felt for Ruth. He had the elders to witness that he would redeem the land and take Ruth as his wife.

Your passion can cause you to form covenants that are Godly and pure, but when left undirected by the Spirit of God, and left uncontrolled, your passions can cause you to form unholy covenants as well. You must guard well your passion and make sure it is always tempered by the Word of God and by the presence of God in your life.

COVENANT OF PROMISE

The last covenant we will look at in this process of redemption is the covenant of promise. It was one thing for Boaz to sit in the gates of the city and make transactions with a group of men, but it was another for him to form that covenant of marriage with Ruth.

The promise of redemption carried with it the responsibility to provide for those that were redeemed. When Boaz redeemed Ruth, that redemption promised her a future. It promised her the opportunity to have a family. It promised her a home and stability. She would never again have to fend for herself. She would never again have to glean in the field. She would never again have to work the threshing floor. Boaz had no other wives, so all that belonged to Boaz now belonged to her as well and to her offspring.

This is what separates Christianity from all the other religions of the world. Buddha did not redeem you. He did not sacrifice himself for you. You are expected to sacrifice to him. The Dalai Lama has not redeemed you. Joseph Smith,

Mary Bakker Eddy, Mohammad, nor any other figure that was worshiped had the power to redeem. Satan himself could not redeem, rather he plunder what had already been purchased through the cross. Jesus has redeemed you and with that redemption came with his promise that he will never to leave you nor forsake you. You have his promise of healing, of provision, of blessing, of instruction, and of direction, because he has paid the price of your redemption.

You may have lived in Moab where you did not know what had been provided to you through redemption, but now you are an heir of God and a joint heir with Jesus Christ the Son of God.

Out of that covenant of promise between Boaz and Ruth came a child whose name was Obed. Obed had a son by the name of Jessie who had a son by the name of David who would rise to rule over Judah and eventually over all of Israel.

You cannot separate redemption from promise, nor can you separate covenant and promise. They are forever joined. Redemption apart from promise, passion, provision, and potential is merely a transaction. When you redeem something, you protect what has been redeemed with all of your might.

You have been redeemed. You have been bought with a price and paid for in full. Fulfill the purpose for which you were redeemed. Fulfill your potential with the gifts and talents God has provided you with and the passion that lies within you. You will discover that all the promises He has made to you will come to pass because He keeps his covenants.

By herself, Ruth would have starved to death in Judah. She would have always been looked upon as a stranger and an outsider, but because of her covenant with Naomi, she was accepted. That was the strength and the power of that covenant.

THE RIGHT OF RELATIONSHIP

One of the most powerful themes we discover in these few short chapters that make up the Book of Ruth is the theme of relationship. Stop and think for just a moment—where will your life would be without the relationships you have forged, and the value they have added to your life. One of the most basic needs, we as humans have, is the need of relationship. The need for one another. We were not built to be independent, but rather inter-dependant. People claim to be *independently wealthy* or to be a *self-made man*. That's not true. They had goods or services they sold to others, so it was others who made them wealthy. Yes, they supplied the ideas and the business savvy but without the participation of others they would have never seen wealth. The same is true with those who claim to be *self-made*. They are what they are by the grace of God and because of the influence of others in their life.

When you have a relationship with someone, especially by blood, there are certain rights that come with and because of that relationship that others who are not blood-kin do not enjoy.

I remember back in the early '90s, when we were traveling evangelists, I would often drive through West Texas where my parents lived. They gave me a key to their home so I could stop in as I passed through whether they were there or not. I could go to their home, unlock the door, help myself to whatever food may be there, and even spend the night. I had the right to do that because of relationship. Through his lifetime, my father had made hundreds of close friendships, but even though they were acquainted, they did not have the same rights that those who were related had. The relationship of blood gives us the right of access and entrance, not just the right of approach. Anyone has the right of approach, but the blood gives us entrance.

Naomi was related to Boaz. She was his relative. She had the right of entrance. Ruth was a Moabite. An outsider. A stranger. Yes, she had been married to Naomi's son, but she was still a Moabite. When she told Naomi that *your people will be my people and your God shall be my God*, all of that changed. With that statement she forsook her homeland, her people, her false gods, her old family ties. She bound herself by covenant to her new life and these new people. When Boaz took her as his wife, she was no longer an outsider, but now had entrance because of relationship.

One of the things that made Boaz truly unique was his relationship with those who worked for him. He was a kind, compassionate man to all who knew him. He was a man who valued relationship.

There are two key ingredients to a successful relationship—loyalty or faithfulness, and communication. These key ingredients are severely lacking in homes and in churches today. Loyalty is almost a thing of the past. And the church world is no better at it than the secular world. We divorce as often, we have the same problems raising children, we cause the same problems at work, and we change churches at the drop of a hat and are dishonest about our reasons for doing so.

Loyalty is a by-product of trust. When there are no trust issues, loyalty is easy to pledge, but when trust has been destroyed, the level of loyalty decreases significantly. Loyalty does not diminish though just because a family, a business, or a church goes through difficult times. Loyalty demands commitment. They cannot be separated.

Loyalty is not conditional in its truest form. It does not run off at the first sign of conflict or in the heat of battle. Loyalty is not self-preserving, but rather is self-sacrificing.

Boaz was a loyal man. He was loyal to his workers even in times of famine. He was faithful to give even when his harvests may not have been as plentiful. He was faithful to love even when the recipient of his love was from another land.

If you want to build strong relationships in your life, be loyal to those you are in relationship with. Make yourself a valuable part of the lives of those with whom you share relationship. This includes your spouse, your children, your extended family, as well as your friends and co-workers.

When I see people who have difficulty staying employed, one of my first questions is are they loyal? Loyalty buys a great deal of grace and favor from those in authority over you and from those you walk in relationship with.

One of the most endearing qualities Boaz saw in Ruth was her loyalty to Naomi. That loyalty is what caused him to leave her extra grain to glean. It secured her future with Boaz, and that same grace was extended to Naomi because of Ruth's loyalty.

Let's face it. True relationship requires loyalty. A friend who is not loyal is not really a friend. Loyalty does not mean they will always agree with you. It *does* mean however, that they will not allow disagreements to dissolve the relationship.

The second key ingredient in any relationship in order for it to be successful is communication. More marriages are destroyed because of the lack of communication or the inability to communicate clearly, than for any other reason. People cite *irreconcilable differences* all the time in front of the judge who then grants them their divorce decree. What they are saying is—we do not know how to communicate well enough to resolve our conflicts, or we no longer care enough to even try to communicate."

With the increase of technology, communication seems easier than ever. Fax, email, texting, and instant messaging have all but replaced the actual art of speaking. Relationships cannot be built or grow without people actually talking to one another.

Communication is not just speaking however, it is also listening. Not just hearing the words with your ears, but understanding the meaning of those words in your heart.

Boaz was a skilled communicator. He sat at the city gate with ten elders and negotiated the purchase of Naomi's land, and the right to have Ruth as his wife. He was trusted by the men in his city because he was a man of his word.

Boaz was able to walk in his desire and walk in his destiny because he was able to clearly state what that destiny was. He knew God's will for his life and he spoke that will by faith. He had already made the decision in his mind to marry Ruth before he ever met with the elders at the city gate. He knew that was God's plan for his life. But he was willing to speak it out, and as he spoke it, he began to walk in it.

It is vital to our walk with God that we are very careful what we say and how we say it. Someone once said, "Be careful what you murmur when you pray…you might just get what you are asking for."

I will never forget the story my seventh grade science teacher, Mr. Jackson, told us one day in class that emphasizes this point. His neighbor had chickens. Lots of chickens. These chickens made noise all throughout the night to the point that Mr. Jackson was losing sleep. After many nights of this, in a fit of anger one night he said, "God, I wish all those chickens would just die." The next morning, he woke up to discover that God had answered his prayer. All the chickens were dead. The words he had spoken in frustration to God the night before came roaring back to his mind. He went to the neighbors home, shared with them what he had said, and purchased new chickens for the coop to replace those that had died.

I remember the emotion with which he shared that story and the impact it made on his life. We must be careful what we say to one another and how we say it. Our words contain the power of life and death. Be a giver of life!

The words Boaz spoke were words of life to Ruth and Naomi. Because he spoke up for her and redeemed her, land that would have remained unfruitful was plowed, planted, and harvested. Ruth's womb that would have remained barren gave birth to the grandfather of King David. All of this because one day while working his fields, Boaz saw a woman going about her job of gleaning, and he asked, "Who is this woman?" Had he remained quiet, the story may not have ended the same, but he spoke. And because he spoke, Ruth became a part of the lineage of Christ. His words gave her relationship and all the rights that go with it.

From the beginning of time, all God wanted with man was a relationship. When He walked with Adam in the garden in the cool of the day He was seeking relationship. When man sinned, that relationship was broken. We needed a redeemer to take away the curse of sin, and restore our relationship with God. When Jesus gave His life on the cross, He made it possible for us to have that relationship.

One cannot have a relationship with God unless they acknowledge their sins to God, and accept Jesus Christ as their Lord and Savior.

That relationship comes with rights and privileges. We have the right to be called the son's of God. We have the right of inheritance. We have heaven as our eternal reward. We have the right of healing, the right of health, and the right of prosperity in all areas of our lives. We have the right of household salvation. Those rights come because He is now our Father. He redeemed us with the blood of Jesus. The price was paid for our sin. All we have to do is receive and accept that work for ourselves, and live our lives to glorify God.

One of the great things about a healthy relationship is that there are wonderful benefits attached to it. Spiritually speaking, there are blessings and favor that come from having a healthy relationship with God. But understand, you cannot have a terrible relationship with others and have a healthy relationship with God. For your relationship with God to be what it needs to be, you need to have peaceful, healthy relationships with those God has placed in your life. Do everything possible to keep discord, division, and disunity from coming into your life. Keep your relationships pure and whole. And as a result, the blessing on you will be able to flow freely from you into the lives of those you meet. You can have the same blessing and the same kind of favor on you that was on this great, humble man of God we know as Boaz.

BIBLIOGRAPHY PAGE

New International Version. (Colorado Springs); Biblica, 2011 BibleGateway.com. Web. Mar. 2011

The Amplified Bible Expanded Edition. The Zondervan Corporation and The Lockman Foundation. 1987

"I Have Decided to Follow Jesus" S. Sundar Singh – public domain

Merriam-Webster.com. Web 2013 Merriam-Webster, Inc.

"Redeemed" words by Fanny J. Crosby, music by William J. Kirkpatrick